For Annabelle,
Here's to all the breakfasts, brunches, lunches, dinners
and snacks we've had, and the many yet to come.xxxx – E.A.

For Joshua & Sebastian,
who are FAR less messy than a Unicorn – M.B.

Published in the UK by Scholastic, 2022
Euston House, 24 Eversholt Street, London, NW1 1DB
Scholastic Ireland, 89E Lagan Road, Dublin Industrial Estate,
Glasnevin, Dublin, D11 HP5F

SCHOLASTIC and associated logos are trademarks and/or
registered trademarks of Scholastic Inc.

Text © Emma Adams, 2022
Illustrations © Mike Byrne, 2022

The right of Emma Adams and Mike Byrne to be identified
as the author and illustrator of this work has been asserted by them
under the Copyright, Designs and Patents Act 1988.

HB ISBN 9780702318016
PB ISBN 9780702307034

A CIP catalogue record for this book is available from the British Library.

All rights reserved.
This book is sold subject to the condition that it shall not, by way of trade or otherwise, be lent,
hired out or otherwise circulated in any form of binding or cover other than that in which it is published.
No part of this publication may be reproduced, stored in a retrieval system, or transmitted
in any form or by any other means (electronic, mechanical, photocopying, recording or otherwise)
without prior written permission of Scholastic Limited.

Printed in Italy
Paper made from wood grown in sustainable forests and other controlled sources

3 5 7 9 10 8 6 4 2

This is a work of fiction. Names, characters, places, incidents and dialogues are products of the author's imagination
or are used fictitiously. Any resemblance to actual people, living or dead, events or locales is entirely coincidental.

www.scholastic.co.uk

MIX
Paper from
responsible sources
FSC® C023419

The Unicorn Who Came to Breakfast

Emma Adams   Mike Byrne

SCHOLASTIC

I have a story you should know –
it happened not that long ago.
You see, though there was Dad and me,
the two of us would soon be three . . .

That day was rainy – cloudy too.
I was quite **bored** and feeling **blue**,
then,

rat-a-tat

went our front door.
Who could it be?
Who was it for?

I pulled the door wide open, then
heard my dad laugh once, and again.

A unicorn!
Oh wow!
Oh look!

In all that rain,
his long mane shook.

Not big, not small –
unicorn-sized.
My dad and I
were quite surprised.

He said, "I'm lost, nowhere to go.
It's really rather cold, you know.
So, please, could I just come inside?
I'll leave as soon as I have dried."

I stared at him, he stared at me,
then said,

**"Please, can I have
some tea?"**

Oh yes – some tea, how rude of me.
I sat down and we smiled with glee.
"Some breakfast for you?" my dad said,
and Unicorn nodded his head.

He sat down too, and glanced across the table top. "I'm at a loss," he said. "Perhaps just something small..." But then Unicorn

ATE
IT
ALL!

He took some toast
and spread jam thick.

"Don't over-do it,
that's the trick."

Some croissants here,

some butter there
(I think it went into his hair).

Then

munch,

crunch,

crunch

and he was

done.

my dad and I had eaten ...

none!

Then Unicorn let out a sigh
and said, "Thank you. Now, as I dry,
perhaps there's something we could do –
some **crafts** or **games**, just one or two..."

We pulled the games
down from the shelf,
then Unicorn
forgot himself.

"I love this one!"

he shouted out
as pieces scattered all about.

He spied our books, and made a plea:
"How marvellous! Please, read to me?"

We started off
with one,

then two –

yes, unicorns love books.

Who knew?

"What's next?" he said. "Oh, let's do MORE!"
He cantered through the nearest door.
Then found my room and cried out, "PAINT!"
I started to feel slightly faint.

"Be careful of the mess!" I said,
as he sat painting on my bed.

Then suddenly, without a care,
he pointed his nose in the air
and said, "Goodness, what IS that smell?
Can I stay here for LUNCH as well?"

To the kitchen! There we saw
a thing that made us stare in awe . . .

A feast! A table full of treats!
My dad had made such tasty eats!

"Do take a seat," he said and smiled.
I stood, amazed –
this day was wild!

Then Uni said, "You're quite the host –
all of these things I **love** the most!
Though, as I need to eat in haste,
I'll only have a little taste . . ."

A mouthful here, a taster there,
the unicorn sat in a chair,
and said, "Could you please pass a plate?
I'll eat one thing – or maybe eight."

He piled things up, he stacked them on,
then – in a flash – the food was gone.
So he got more! He ate with style
and my dad watched him with a smile.

"I probably should leave,"
he said.
"My friend is waiting . . .
pass the bread?"

So Unicorn didn't stop there,
he picked up berries and a pear.

"Oh, this is SUCH delicious stuff,"
he said, admiring one cream puff

and scoffing sausage rolls with flair.

"Is that a **party ring,**
just there?"

He oo'd and ah'd, he rubbed his tum –
he didn't even leave a crumb.

He said,

"That TRULY was delish.
The cake, the nibbles –
EVERY dish!"

But then, "Oh gosh, I'm **very late!**"
He handed me his empty plate
and called, "**It's really time I hurried,**
no doubt my friend will be quite worried.
You've been SO kind. Goodbye!" he said,
as thunder rumbled overhead.

We watched him walk off in the rain,
and both called out . . .
"Please come again!"